How to Stay
Alive & Well

Despite Your Doctor
Your Insurance Company
& Your Government

Printed in the United States of America.
ISBN: 978-1-59571-280-6
Library of Congress Control Number: Applied For

Word Association Publishers
205 Fifth Avenue
Tarentum, PA 15084
www.wordassociation.com

How to Stay Alive & Well

Despite Your Doctor
Your Insurance Company
& Your Government

by

Dr. Patrick McNally

Word Association Publishers
Tarentum, Pennsylvania

Contents

Introduction

Congratulations on obtaining this book.
Doing so places you in a category of people who understand that taking responsibility for your own health puts you way ahead of the average person concerning your chances for a long, healthy and happy life.

There are many factors that influence health and longevity. It's not possible to outline all of them in a book of this sort. There's a distinction, too, between intervention and prevention in personal health strategy and professional health care. I've written this book to give you the benefit of over twenty years experience treating thousands of patients who've come to me with health problems and with whom I've counseled to seek out simple, effective methods of resolving health issues and staying alive and well into the future.

A great deal of misinformation comes from those who formulate opinions based on limited information, or from those who have an economic interest in a particular treatment being chosen over another. I will not do that. I'll only give you what I've come to know and what's available as objective discussion, admitting up front that I don't and can't know everything. My bias is to the more natural, drug-free and non surgical approaches to health care, and my intention is that this book can serve as stimulation that you might choose for yourself what to pursue and what to avoid in the enjoyment of good health. The information here is also relative to the current health care environment, typical health insurance allowances and limitations, personal injury insurance and available data from independent research and other sources.

The focus on health insurance in my title is important for two reasons: First, most persons seeking health care in the United States want to use their health insurance, auto med-pay policy or Medicare depending on circumstance. The type of insurance that may apply depends on circumstance and need. Second, I want to give people what they want, and if being a provider on insurance contracts helps I'll do so in the best ways available now. It's my policy to keep our fees reasonable for all patients, those with and without insurance. A significant challenge today is that the insurance industry has been decreasing reimbursement of claims over many years while simultaneously increasing co-pay and deductibles. On the one hand the increased deductibles and co-payments hurt the consumer, and on the other hand decreased reimbursements hurt the provider (this is why so many doctors are dropping certain insurance contracts). You need to know how to maneuver through this maze of insurance policies and changing provisions to make the best choices for yourself and your family. As the United States has become increasingly "insurance dependent" we've not seen an improvement in health care with reduction in costs as predicted. As a friend who's also providing health care services recently said to me, "managed care has become mangled care." It's a major problem in our country now, but you do have choices and can direct your own health outcomes in many ways.

You may or may not have been the victim of insurance bad faith or denial of claims. Certainly you've heard the stories, and myriad books and movies are available with this as a plot.[1] I want to let you know what you can do when it comes to that, or how you might support your health care providers so there's little or no liability to you for additional amounts an insurance company may deny. The Ohio Department of Insurance states it this way:

"Claim denials from insurance companies were the number one complaint of Ohio insurance con-

sumers in 2007, according to statistics released by the Ohio Department of Insurance. Nearly one-third of the 7,140 consumer complaints received by the Department dealt with the denial of claims by insurance companies. There were 312 more consumer complaints filed in 2007, up from 6,828 complaints in 2006." [2]

If this is true for one state it may also be true for many or all. Some states make available these statistics and some do not.

THE DAWN OF PERSONALIZED MEDICINE: THE SELF DIRECTED PATIENT

If we listen to insurance companies and politicians it sounds like good health is dependent on some form of contracted "coverage." What does this mean? It's hard to say for sure, and it's not my intent here to assign motives to anyone, because I don't and can't know what others' motives are. But it seems clear that to allow insurance carriers to contract with every U.S. citizen is an opening for increasing control by the insurance companies, not less. Is this what we want? Personally I suspect it would create more problems than it solves. At the end of this book you'll find a discussion of my proposed solutions to these problems. Does having an insurance contract guarantee that you'll get the care you need, or that you're protected from financial liability? One group puts it this way:

"Claims denial has reached an all time high, and consequently insurance companies have suddenly increased their refusal to fulfill claims by their policyholders... Many insurance companies want to limit their liability...." [3]

Health plans and providers are under pressure to accommodate demands being made from health care consumers. Statistics demonstrate that patients want more communication from their doctors, including easy access to questions answered by email. But doctors have dragged their feet when it comes to providing accessibility in this way. Many intermediaries have intervened in the form of websites as sources of information, with inherent biases, that provide the opportunity for personal research into previously esoteric aspects of health care such as laboratory test results, second opinions and alternative options. A major attribute of this movement is the need to perceive value for services received. Consumers want to know where the most value can be had, which has driven pharmaceutical and insurance companies to entrench position in the marketplace deeper and deeper. Clever marketing tries to paint a picture of value even in the context of potentially serious, sometimes life threatening side effects.

Research conducted into the emerging health care environment by Forrester Research, Inc. suggests that personalized medicine is forcing the creation of new and different models of health care delivery. Of importance is the idea of integrating myriad professional orientations while networking between these various providers with best outcome for patients. This idea, though, finds great resistance while established orthodoxy and big business try to maintain a hold on how health care is delivered and to whom under particular circumstances.

The self directed health care consumer is one who refuses to accept the old balance of power in which insurance companies and doctors direct, often without full disclosure, the procedures and treatments recommended or applied. Speaking for myself, I very much respect self direction in choosing options to stay healthy. Value for the self directed patient or health care consumer centers on achieving goals within a reasonable time and without adverse side effects.

The persistent downward trends in insurance and Medicare reimbursement are, again, challenging to the business of providing health care and don't always support the self directed patient. I've said many times to my patients and friends: *People don't need "coverage", they need care.* I mean simple and straight forward, effective and reasonable, proven self and health care that saves money while rendering a positive, fast result. By the way, there's a big difference between "alive and well" and suppressing symptoms with drugs (more on this later).

The following is an example of how health care dollars are wasted because an insurance contract has primary influence on where and how a patient seeks treatment: In my profession there are studies that demonstrate efficacy of preventive care for spinal health issues along with education that saves people suffering and money. This, though, surprisingly does not change the way in which patients with back pain are treated or referred through the health care network of licensed providers. Consider the following study:

In the early 90's Saco Defense Corporation (later purchased by General Dynamics) wanted to find out if they could save money on back related injuries, lost wages and insurance premiums by introducing a program of education and preventive care. The results were telling.[4]

In 1990 there were *304% higher* incidence of lost days from work and *50 times* the cost in terms of insurance premiums without preventive care and education of workers to avoid spinal injury than with preventive care. If this is true, why then would it not become routine health care policy to recommend to patients experiencing or vulnerable to back pain, spinal injury or arthritis that preventive care is statistically helpful? Again, I won't assign motives, only point to the studies and history that can assist you to make the best choices for your personal self and health care now and for the future. Suffice to say here that there's competition for health care dollars just as there is for money in every industry. If, though, you know that one mode of care is proven more effective than another, or you have information that can help you make the necessary choices that provide effective treatment without side effects, you are again to be congratulated for the foresight and responsibility this demonstrates.

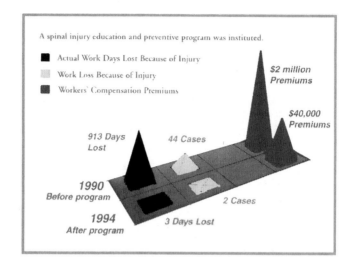

A spinal injury education and preventive program was instituted.

■ Actual Work Days Lost Because of Injury

  Work Loss Because of Injury

■ Workers' Compensation Premiums

913 Days Lost

44 Cases

$2 million Premiums

$40,000 Premiums

1990
Before program

1994
After program

3 Days Lost

2 Cases

CASE HISTORY #1: CAR CRASH VICTIM GOES A YEAR IN SEVERE PAIN BEFORE THE RIGHT REFERRAL IS MADE.

(All cases cited are examples from our files. Names and personal details are changed to protect privacy.)

Tony L. was 54 when a drunk driver plowed into the back of his car while he was stopped at a stop light on the way home from dinner with friends. The crash was so hard that his car was totaled, and he was taken to the emergency room right away. He had pain in his neck and back, numbness in his left arm and hand, with severe headaches too. After receiving a brief examination and given a prescription he was told to "see an orthopedist" if his pain did not go away in a few days. Not only did the pain persist, it got worse until Tony couldn't tolerate it. He did seek out an orthopedic doctor and began treatment with medication including muscle relaxants and physical therapy. X-ray and MRI showed nothing broken, dislocated or herniated. Therefore no surgery was indicated and the doctor kept him on medication and going to therapy. But Tony's pain did not go away. After a few weeks he quit the therapy, continuing to swallow the prescription drugs to "take the edge off" so that he could continue working. He couldn't, though, exercise or enjoy his favorite sport: golf. Driving in his car for more than an hour also caused flair-ups of back pain.

After a year and more than $10,000.00 in medical costs (most covered by his insurance), in desperation he asked his primary care doctor to refer him to me. My staff and I performed a thorough examination and found that Tony suffered from chiropractic subluxation (more commonly called "misalignment") of spinal bones and joints with spasm of muscles and pinched nerves. Tony's headaches had gotten so bad he had trouble sleeping and sometimes missed a day at work. He was terribly frustrated when we first met.

We carefully explained to Tony that the abnormal alignment of the bones and joints of his neck and back, which did show up on the x-rays but were considered unimportant to the medical doctors, was the cause of the now chronic muscle spasms and pinched nerves that caused so much pain and restricted his lifestyle. He seemed to understand when we explained that the chronic spasms were his body's response as protection against damage at the level of his spine. Tony began a series of treatments to his neck and back. He received physical therapy modalities including electrical muscle stimulation and therapeutic ultrasound along with chiropractic adjusting techniques to relieve pressure on nerves. Within a few treatments he was reporting significant improvement, and after a few more he was able to drive without pain and once more enjoy a few rounds of golf. The only remaining negative for Tony was his utter frustration that someone had not referred him earlier for the care that could have saved him a year of pain.

The United States Department of Commerce keeps track of income for specific professions correlating with documentation of cost for certain services. The following diagram illustrates.[5]

Spinal Adjustments Not Only Make People Healthier, It Costs Less For Everyone, Including Insurance Companies and You

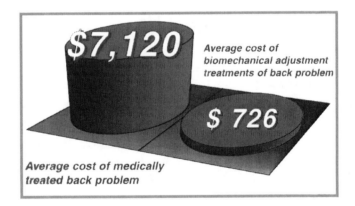

$7,120 Average cost of biomechanical adjustment treatments of back problem

$ 726

Average cost of medically treated back problem

LET'S TAKE A LOOK AT ANOTHER ISSUE OF IMPORTANCE FOR MAINTAINING GOOD HEALTH NUTRITION: THINGS HAVE GOTTEN WORSE

Many people are confused about nutrition, and with good reason! What I said above about misinformation being the result of limitations of available understanding is likely nowhere more blatant than in the area of nutrition and advice coming from "professionals" about the foods we eat. Anyone who's had a few days in a hospital can probably attest to the fact that modern medicine puts little to no importance on myriad studies available to suggest that food is an ultra important contributor to or detractor from our health. I try to read one or two books a year about diet and nutrition, and I can tell you that opinions are many and diverse. My intention here is to help you become more aware that you might learn something of value that can help you stay alive and well.

Since 2000 medical doctors have started giving more advice in the area of nutrition, but have they read the studies and the books? What's their interest and education in topics of nutrition? Maybe you'd agree that it's helpful to have a clue what your doctor knows, what his or her true areas of expertise really are. Why don't medical doctors engage the important issue of nutrition more often?

"Which 'sensible diet' do you want me to follow? I found 123,942 of them on the internet!"

"Unfortunately, many of them [medical doctors] don't know much about nutrition. When getting nutrition advice from a health professional, please choose one carefully. Under the Federal law known as DSHEA, only a health care professional, especially a doctor, can give nutrition advice. However, a research poster on nutrition education in medical schools shows that most doctors have gotten only a day of education about nutrition during medical school..."[6]

Chiropractic physicians, in addition to being generally more interested in issues of holistic health care, related health care modalities, and integrative medicine, receive an education that might surprise you.

"Chiropractors receive much of the same education as our medical counterparts... Chiropractors actually receive more hours of instruction in the basic sciences, as well as over 600 hours in the diagnosis of medical conditions. Three years of radiology, 2 years of neurology, more hours in orthopedics and anatomy and are required to pass 4 different national board examinations prior to graduation... The average chiropractor receives close to 5,000 hours of instruction... With close to two years of education in nutrition, chiropractors are among the most highly educated doctors in the health field. Compare that to an average of 25 hours or less of nutrition being taught to medical doctors and you begin to see the problem..." [7]

Let's take a look at how nutrition has changed for the worse and valuable information that might help you stay healthy. Using spinach as an example of how foods can be altered: Polluted air, chemicals and pesticides have lead to the depletion of minerals in the soil, radically reducing the fundamental nutritional value of fruits and vegetables.[8]

In this context nutritionists generally urge whole, non-synthetic vitamin supplements to promote better health. The popular idea that a diversified diet will provide all necessary nutrients may no longer apply. If taking supplements, it's also important to consider solubility. Most people don't realize that "one a day" does little to enhance the cellular environment in the body with important nutrients, especially when levels may have been low for awhile. Certain vitamins are water soluble, others fat soluble. For the water soluble variety it's more effective to take them more than once a day, sometimes over the course of the day, to be sure levels are high enough to support health at the cellular level. No specific recommendations are made here for any particular disorders or needs, only a suggestion that self education regarding vitamin supplementation might prove an enhancement to your self and health care strategy. One source, one opinion, is never enough to make a clear decision. It's important to self educate in a way that will support and promote your best health possible while also considering your uniqueness and the needs expressed through personal idiosyncrasies. There may also be subtle but important interactions of nutrients and drugs to be considered. Ask your medical doctor if he or she knows of any reason you should not take a certain vitamin in combination with any prescription medication.

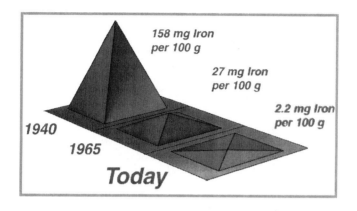

158 mg Iron per 100 g

27 mg Iron per 100 g

2.2 mg Iron per 100 g

1940

1965

Today

THE RIGHT 'PLACE' FOR YOUR DOCTOR OR THERAPIST

As licensed by the Virginia Board of Medicine and under Virginia Code § 8.01-66.12 I'm entitled to use the phrase "Chiropractic Physician" to describe the services I render by my license. Also, the State Board in Maryland in 1985 identified my license to practice as "Doctor of Chiropractic" with certification in physical therapy added. Through these past 23 years of providing health care I've come to know just where my place is. When a patient comes to me, and I accept their case in a professional capacity, the only effective place for me to take is at the last position in his or her life and in the complexity of interpersonal relationships he or she enjoys. What I mean by this is that to take a higher position, assume an air of authority, of knowing more than one does, or imposing recommendations without considering all the aspects of need and circumstance, a subtle principle of service is violated. I call it 'being out of order,' something that doesn't provide the best possible healing environment. The only way to truly heal is with an attitude of humility, which most of us (including me) must cultivate as it doesn't always come easily. The good news is that my scope of practice is narrow enough that I can be good at it while trusting my patients to inform me of their perceptions about how much care they may or may not need at any given time. If patient and doctor work together to discover what's most effective it's gratifying for both while supporting the self directed patient.

My point here is that in our health care environment we seem to have a problem. The bottom line often subverts the best interests of the patient, and humility is often abandoned (see bibliography reference to *Critical Condition: How Health Care in America Became Big Business—and Bad Medicine* and *Selling Sickness: How the World's Biggest Pharmaceutical Companies Are Turning Us All Into Patients*). We've all heard the stories of the $10 q-tip in the hospital and the scandals with FDA approved drugs that do harm. Can we make another choice? The following story illustrates an important issue.

"At the beginning of the twentieth century, a doctor named Knock started to exorcise the healthiness from his patients. The Frenchman longed for a world that contained only patients: 'Every well person is a sick person who doesn't know it.'

Knock put his theory into practice in a mountain village called Saint Maurice. The residents were in good health and didn't go to the doctor. The old country doctor, the impoverished Dr. Parpalaid, tried to console his successor and said to him: 'Here you have the best kind of clientele: one is left in peace.' Knock wasn't going to accede to this.

But how was the new doctor going to lure people into his [practice]? What was it he was going to prescribe to the healthy? Knock cunningly flatters the village teacher and gets him to give the residents talks about the alleged dangers of micro-organisms. He engages the village drummer and induces him to announce that the new doctor invites all residents to a free consultation – 'in order to prevent the perilous spread of all kinds of diseases now circulating in our once so healthy region.' The waiting room is getting crowded.

During [practice] hours Knock diagnoses peculiar symptoms and hammers into the guileless villagers that they are in need of his constant care. From then on many stay in bed and restrict their intake to a little water. Fi-

nally, the whole village seems to be one big hospital. There remain just enough healthy people to look after the ill. The pharmacist becomes a rich man; the same goes for the landlord, whose pub, transformed into a makeshift infirmary, is fully occupied at all times.[9]

Who's responsible for the fate of these people? Is it the doctor, the pharmacist, the advertisers or the villagers themselves? There are many levels of liability in such a scenario, and the villagers allowed themselves to be duped, you might say. In the absolute sense each of us is responsible for our own lives. It reminds of that old saying; "Fool me once, shame on you. Fool me twice, shame on me." Effective self and health care requires awareness on the part of people in general regarding true principles of health, and the discrimination to avoid that which is unnecessary in the pursuit of good health and quality of life. Where, for instance, is discrimination if we believe prime time advertising for pharmaceutical drugs that carry multiple side effects but are offered up in smiling, happy, colorful strategies? Sometimes a drug is advertised without even referring to what it's been approved for. Have you noticed? If more people had this awareness we likely would not have as much being spent in the U.S. today on health care with no end to the rising costs in sight. The following image depicts cost in billions until today. [10]

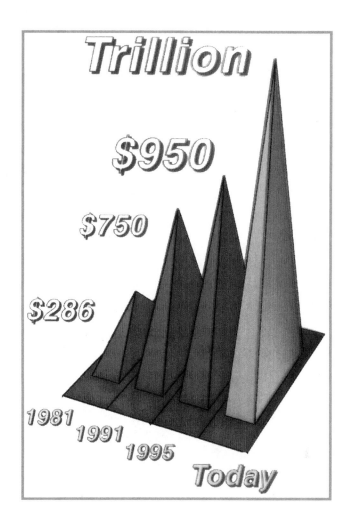

"So many people spend their health gaining wealth, and then have to spend their wealth to regain health."
A.J. Reb Materi

Why are we seeing such escalating health care costs? Are we being wrongly influenced or 'duped' into this situation? Fred Fiske gives regular commentaries on National Public Radio. Here's one of interest to this discussion:

"We went to one of the superstore pharmacies last week to fill one of my wife's prescriptions... The price was $121.00, just about $4.00 a capsule. When I lamented the high price, the pharmacist suggested that we buy the generic, at $19.21, and not for thirty but for ninety [20 cents per pill]. ... We're appalled by Medicare's prohibition from negotiating drug prices with suppliers as Medicaid and VA can. ... And here in the U.S., we buy generic whenever possible. Sometimes, though, we must go to Canada for generics that are not available in the U.S. So we looked into the reason why a U.S. branded drug was available as a generic in Canada but not here. And the reason is beyond belief. In the United States pharmaceutical companies are paying off generic drug makers not to produce generic versions of expensive branded drugs. The FTC ostensibly started looking into this almost two years ago, but has anything been done to stop these anti-competition agreements? No way!

In the same vein was a recent article noting that U.S. prosecutors settled a case against four orthopedic devise manufacturers for a mere $311,000,000.00. What was the basis for the suit? That in a four year period these manufacturers of artificial hips and knees had paid out over $800,000,000.00 to orthopedic surgeons in return for the surgeons' continued use of their specific products. Seems to me that the doctors made out pretty well. And for a mere $311,000,000.00 the manufacturers were able to control three quarters of a nine plus billion dollar industry.

... I'm revolted that our health care system has been hijacked by greed and indifference in the name of a free market. And I wonder where Congress is in all of this. Think about that next time you pay four dollars for a twenty cent pill." [11]

CASE HISTORY #2:
YOUNG WOMAN SCARED TO TEARS AFTER BEING MISDIAGNOSED BY HER MEDICAL DOCTOR

Jenny B. was only 32 when she arrived in my office in a state of despair. She had numbness and tingling sensations into her right arm that got worse during the night, causing her to wake up and shift positions. There was no trauma or other cause of her problem. Jenny was most concerned because her medical doctor had suggested that she was suffering from the beginning stages of multiple sclerosis and would need many tests to make the diagnosis with likely long term medical intervention. She broke into tears as she told me her story.

But Jenny also didn't completely accept this negative suggestion. She wanted to have an opinion other than in medical circles, so she came to me as an alternative. She seemed open minded and receptive to looking at her condition in a different way. We proceeded conservatively to find out if there could be another cause of Jenny's problem.

After a thorough examination including x-rays, I told Jenny that in my opinion her symptoms were coming from a slight disc bulge (slipped disc) in her neck. The reason I felt confident was also based on the fact that her symptoms were not generalized as in the more serious issue of MS, only effecting one arm, and that she could change her symptoms by shifting position. This pointed to a condition of a pinched nerve at the level of her spine directly causing the pain and numbness. The simplest approach was to relieve the pressure on the nerve and see if it helped.

After just five treatments in my office Jenny reported significant improvement. It was then obvious that she wasn't suffering from the beginning stages of MS, and she gave a deep sigh of relief. She told me she thought the medical doctor had "jumped the gun" by assigning her symptoms to a disease without a full examination first. I told her that the medical doctor meant no harm, he just assumed the worst. Jenny received a total of 12 treatments from me after which her symptoms were completely gone and didn't come back.

The amount of time and money saved in Jenny's case is impossible to calculate. Her willingness to try something unusual for her is what saved whatever amount that would have been. Good for Jenny and for her insurance companies.

THIS BOOK IS NOT MEDICAL ADVICE: THE CHOICE IS YOURS ALONE

The goal of this book is to give you information about self and health care strategies that might be right for you. But you must make the choice. You may do well to remain open to various options to make the best use of your free will in achieving and maintaining your health goals. From my side, I may be able to help, but only after you and I have decided that there's a good chance my knowledge and experience serves your highest interests. **I do not accept cases that my experience, expertise, license and discrimination in-**

dicate as outside my ability to help. Alternatives to standard care are increasingly popular, and my office supports through referral many providers with whom we've come to trust and know their level of professionalism and capacity. At your request we work closely with any and all providers from whom you're receiving treatment or with whom you may work while seeing us. The interest in alternative medicine has risen over many years, with good reason to believe it can compliment many approaches already in place.

"Alternative (aka complimentary, unconventional, unorthodox, integrative) therapies encompass a broad spectrum of practices and beliefs. From the standpoint of medical sociology they may be defined as practices that are not in conformity to the beliefs and standards of the dominant group of medical practitioners in a society. Two national surveys conducted in the United States have functionally defined alternative... as 'interventions neither taught widely in U.S. medical schools nor generally available in U.S. hospitals.' Ernst et al. contend that complimentary medicine is diagnosis, treatment and/or prevention which complements mainstream medicine by contributing to a common whole, by satisfying a demand not met by orthodoxy or by diversifying the conceptual frameworks of medicine." [12]

CONSIDER THE WAYS IN WHICH EVERY PART OF YOUR BODY IS CONNECTED TO EVERY OTHER PART

Let's say you have pain in the right leg below the knee without pain in any other area of your body. Maybe it's difficult to walk, or you have cramps in that leg at times. The tendency is to think the pain is a localized problem, maybe a torn muscle or tendon. That's reasonable, and it's important to rule out various causes of pain that could be dangerous. If, after doing so, the pain is still there what could be the problem? From the chiropractic point of view that pain may reflect a problem somewhere along the sciatic nerve that originates in the lower spine. With several branches of spinal nerves contributing to the sciatic and literally millions of nerve fibers bundled within the sciatic nerves, if a specific part of the nerve is pinched or irritated, it's possible you'd have pain only in the area below the knee of one leg. To treat only the leg, then, would prove ineffective, and if there's direct pressure on the nerve medication won't usually make it feel much better.

The solution, then, is to directly relieve the pressure on the nerve. Nothing else will cure the problem, and if it's possible to do it without surgery the better. There are many effective techniques to provide relief in this way that avoid surgery and prevent future problems.

There's a drug being marketed now for a condition called "Restless Leg Syndrome" or "RLS." Have you heard of it? Side effects include "nausea, dizziness, somnolence, insomnia, constipation, asthenia, and hallucinations."[13] I question the general necessity of such a drug because many patients have reported improvement of these "restless" symptoms after a few gentle adjustments to the lower back area where the sciatic nerve originates, with no side effects. Pressure on any nerve can cause facilitation, an excitation of the nerve that causes overstimulation to the area where that nerve delivers energy. Is it better to treat the cause or suppress symptoms with potentially dangerous side effects?

Nerves exiting the spinal cord deliver energy to every body part. If too much or too little nerve energy is delivered pain or ill health result. For example, too little nerve energy can result in numbness or weakness. Too much causes pain, muscle spasms, cramping or dysfunction. Keeping pressure from building up around the sensitive spinal nerves is one way of contributing to positive self and health care.

CASE HISTORY #3: INSOMNIA ABATES AFTER CHIROPRACTIC CARE

Ms. Ellie R. came to see me with burning pain in her middle back, localized to the level of the shoulder blades that hurt when she took a deep breath or after sitting at her desk at work for several hours. The pain had been getting worse for several weeks. An x-ray showed an abnormal curve (scoliosis) in that part of Ellie's spine. Because there were no prior x-rays we didn't know if the abnormal curvature had worsened recently. What we did know is that the curve was putting pressure on the rib cage and contributing to painful muscle spasms.

After a few treatments Ellie reported feeling better, able to sit at her desk for longer periods without pain. She also reported a positive side effect: Many years of insomnia was improving significantly. Ellie explained that she had resisted medical suggestions to take prescription sleeping aids because she "doesn't like to take pills." She was very happy about this unexpected result, and looked brighter and healthier too.

I carefully explained to Ellie that insomnia is not a condition that my scope of practice recognizes and that the only condition treated in her case was the cause of back pain, specifically the scoliosis. However, I also explained to Ellie that when spinal nerves are pinched there can be an inability to relax. I told her, from my point of view, that when a person is able to sleep easily there's normally a withdrawal of the energy traveling along nerves to various body parts. We know this because when asleep many people won't be disturbed by normal stimuli (i.e., light and sound), because the nerves are not active. If the energy can't withdraw because of pinched nerves, or even subtle irritation (referring again to facilitation) it becomes difficult to fall asleep.

By treating Ellie's underlying issue we inadvertently corrected for another problem and saved her suffering for the future. It also saved her from taking some powerful drugs that could become addictive.

There are many examples of how the connections within our body can serve to prevent or relieve pain and ill health.

Acupuncture is an ancient form of treatment that finds connections within the body correlating to various body parts. We work with well trained acupuncturists in our area for referral and treatment of patients' needs when appropriate.

"The human body has a bio-energy-circulation system similar to the blood-circulation system. The bio-energy flows along 12 main meridians, or chan-

nels. These are symmetrical on each side of the body, each pair being related to a specific organ...

In disease, imbalances develop in these energy flows, causing some of the transformer points to become irritated or congested. This results in pain or weakness in the surrounding muscles. Stimulating these points with special needles (acupuncture) or pressure (acupressure) helps to normalize impaired conditions. In addition, you may use electro-acupuncture to treat points with a weak DC current." [14]

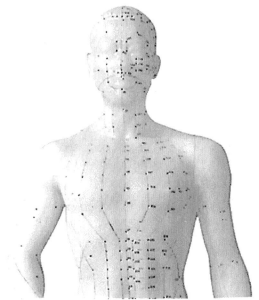

Location of Acupuncture Points and Meridians
(partially demonstrated)

Another example of how the body is connected, one that's powerful but not widely applied, is called reflexology. Like acupuncture it accesses specific locations on the body, called 'reflex' points, to influence health in other body parts. The principle is to increase circulation to body parts through deep reflexive relaxation, thereby promoting optimal health. I've seen many amazing results through this approach, having been trained in my early 20's. In fact, my training in reflexology influenced me directly to the chiropractic profession, and I make myself available to give hands on classes in these techniques to help people help themselves. It's possible through understanding how such connections benefit health to practice self care in a way that may allow for improvement of conditions unresponsive to other types of treatment, and to prevent small health issues turning into much larger problems. How much money do you suppose would be saved in the health care system if doctors truly educated their patients concerning the benefits of these alternatives? Looking for the connections that may influence and positively treat the body is often preferable to looking at the symptoms alone.

Reflexology with Pressure Points on Feet

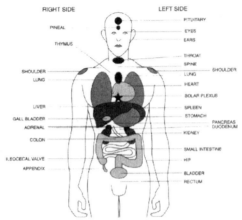

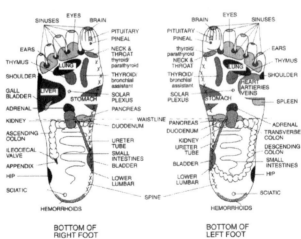

WHY DON'T MEDICAL DOCTORS REFER TO ALTERNATIVE AND COMPLIMENTARY PROVIDERS MORE OFTEN?

In every profession and industry we find competition, differences of opinion, and efforts to control the marketplace. In health care in the U.S. the medical profession, particularly the American Medical Association, and the pharmaceutical industry have tried to influence your decisions for many decades. It's not usually a balanced debate. In the late 70's and into the 80's there was a court case intended to stop violations of anti-trust laws that hurt many well intentioned doctors and patients. Consider the following case that resulted in a decision against the AMA for conspiracy to destroy another profession. [15]

For many years the medical and chiropractic professions were at odds. Medical doctors didn't understand or like the paradigm chiropractors proposed: That the human body, given the right stimulus, is a self healing mechanism. They considered chiropractors unscientific, ignoring decades of success enjoyed by the chiropractic profession, emerging research, patient satisfaction surveys and anecdotal evidence that chiropractic is an effective form of care for many human ailments. The disagreement between the professions became so great as to evoke from the American Medical Association the inception of a committee with the stated aim of eliminating the chiropractic profession. The AMA also instructed medical doctors to boycott chiropractic by making no referrals or working with chiropractic physicians in any way, claiming it as a violation of medical ethics. With these facts in mind a response was proposed and initiated in the courts to defend the chiropractic profession and its right to fair treatment for the benefit of chiropractic patients, people in need, and health care consumers.

The first trial

In 1976, Chester Wilk and three other chiropractors sued the AMA, several nationwide healthcare associations, and several physicians for violations of sections 1 and 2 of the Sherman Antitrust Act. [They] lost at the first trial in 1981, then obtained a new trial on appeal in 1983 because of improper jury instructions and admission of irrelevant and prejudicial evidence (Wilk v. American Medical Ass'n, 735 F.2d 217, 7th Cir. 1983).

The second trial

In the second trial case the AMA had the burden of proof, needing to establish the validity of the boycott... [The AMA] had to show their concern could not have been adequately satisfied in a manner less restrictive of competition...

The resulting trial in May and June of 1987 was a bench trial in which Judge Susan Getzendanner personally heard the evidence and made factual findings.

Judge's findings in the second trial

On September 25, 1987, Judge Susan Getzendanner issued her opinion that the AMA had violated Section 1, but not 2, of the Sherman Act, and that it had engaged in an unlawful conspiracy in restraint of trade "to contain and eliminate the chiropractic profession." (Wilk v. American Medical Ass'n, 671 F. Supp. 1465, N.D. Ill. 1987). She issued a permanent injunction against the AMA under Section 16 of the Clayton Act to prevent such future behavior.

For an overview of how the AMA has influenced health care policy I recommend reading *The Serpent on the Staff: The Unhealthy Politics of the American Medical Association* by Howard Wolinsky and Tom Brune.

"Chicago Sun Times reporters Wolinsky and Brune argue that what is good for the American Medical Association (AMA) is not necessarily good for the public or its

health. Since the AMA is a doctors' organization, few readers will be surprised by the authors' revelations of conflicts of professional vs. public interests. The authors provide an overview of the AMA, discussing its organization and membership and how it works; its political 'wheeling and dealing'; and some of its less altruistic actions regarding alternative (i.e., nonallopathic) medicines, Medicare, and the tobacco and drug industries and its ethical waverings on health issues such as abortion and AIDS. They write that 'the AMA is a cheerleader for just enough reform to avoid a major overhaul' of the U.S. healthcare system. Recommended for healthcare and public policy collections." [16]

CASE HISTORY #4: "I DON'T WANT TO TAKE THESE PILLS ANY LONGER. I JUST FEEL TIRED ALL THE TIME."

Joan S. woke up one day with severe back pain. "I can't even put my socks on without help," she said. There was no injury or identified cause, and no history of back trouble in her life, although she reported that her father experienced severe back pain at times and had ever since she could remember. Joan had been under the care of an orthopedic surgeon and referral to physical therapy, with some but not much relief, even after many weeks of treatment. The doctor had prescribed muscle relaxants and anti-inflam-

*matory medications, which Joan reported were making
her "tired all the time."*

*Reviewing the MRI and other tests Joan brought with
her for our first meeting, there was clear indication of disc
decay in the lower spine. She'd been told there was no need
of surgery, so the doctor prescribed medication and physical therapy instead. The treatments she'd been receiving
were focused on the symptoms in muscles but were doing
nothing to address the underlying problem of disc decay.
Joan was pleased when I explained to her that we've successfully treated thousands of people with this same condition and we could be fairly certain of a good result in her
case. She was also willing to do some simple exercises I'd
prescribe to help her along. She was anxious to get well
and excited to cooperate with my recommendations.*

*We started conservatively and saw Joan twice a week
for the first three weeks, after which she reported feeling
about 50% better. She was thrilled, and able to put her
socks on without help at that point. She asked me if she
should continue taking the medication, to which I replied
"That's between you and your medical doctor. I don't prescribe medication nor tell patients when to stop taking it.
Please call the doctor who prescribed it for that discussion."
After another two weeks of treatment in my office Joan
was able to return to her regular tennis club that she had
missed, and after just three additional treatments the pain*

was completely gone. She had discussed her situation with the medical doctor and been released from his care or need to take medications any longer. The last time I saw Joan she looked energized and happy.

There was only one frustration for Joan as she went through the treatment in our office: Her insurance company limited her chiropractic benefit to just five treatments for any one condition (we consider a fair allowance to be at least 20). When Joan found out about that limitation she made a choice to pay out of pocket for the additional treatments she was going to need to get well. She also told us she was going to shop for better insurance that would give her more visits if she needed to come back to us for any reason in the future.

THE STRUCTURE OF HEALTH CARE REVOLUTIONS

You may recognize my play on words here after the classic book written in 1962, *The Structure of Scientific Revolutions,* by Thomas Kuhn. In it he introduces the concept of a "paradigm shift" and how it occurs in the scientific community. It's no surprise that these shifts occur slowly, usually with the older, established scientists in any particular group holding fast to orthodoxy and the younger, more open minded being receptive to new ideas. But the slow acceptance of new insights has often disallowed the best service to those who would benefit from those insights, and it continues to this day that new paradigms challenging the establishment are disregarded or considered "unscientific" or lacking value. I believe that the health care crisis we're in now requires a revolution of thinking on the part of every person who wants to enjoy high quality of life now and later. In particular, providers are being challenged to shift in ways that support a new paradigm. We might again refer to the "self-directed patient" and the new paradigm embraced in that movement.

Here are a few examples of changes in the paradigm of health care that were at first resisted. Because you accept them as fact now you may be surprised.

1. In 1842 the first practical anesthetic was applied (ether). Before this it was common practice to get the patient drunk to perform an amputation or other surgery. People suffered greatly, but still there was resistance to change and suspicion that this new procedure was dangerous.

2. Louis Pasteur discovered bacteria in 1858. The idea of tiny, invisible bugs that would contribute to disease was difficult to accept for most people then.

3. Daniel David Palmer established the Chiropractic Profession in 1895 after curing Harvey Lillard of deafness. At the time it was considered a miracle, later rejected by medical doctors, and then proven that to relieve certain pressure to the cranial nerves and spinal cord can have this effect.

4. Another revolutionary, Sigmund Freud, in 1906 identified and treated psychosomatic disorders. This was a new idea, controversial and took time for health care to assimilate. Now we know that these are valid and often serious influences to our health. The mind is a powerful thing.

5. The first organ transplant was in 1954. It seemed like science fiction that doctors could perform such an operation. Now we accept it and often marvel at how a person lives a normal life after transplantation.

Today we have the holistic revolution in health care being resisted and often denigrated by an established orthodoxy that cannot seem to accept the simplicity of the model. For instance, homeopathy, a system of health care widely practiced in Europe and Asia, holds that to cure disease the body must "*express* symptoms from the inside out." That is, the symptoms resulting from such processes as toxicity in the body must find expression through the avenues available for a real cure to take place. Modern medicine (allopathy) holds to a model of symptom suppression, forcing the body's mechanisms to push symptoms in rather than out. Hence the pharmaceutical industry's never ending efforts to find the next pill that suppresses this or that symptom. As I've often argued, both paradigms can't be true, they're mutually exclusive. Are there times when suppression is necessary? Sure. But to really be healthy maybe we need to look at different paradigms and apply what has the most potential to support life.

The paradigm in chiropractic, as in other approaches, holds that the body is self healing if given the right support. Any irritation to or compromise of the spine, nerves or proprioceptive functioning, when removed, will provide for healing in myriad ways and for many conditions. For more than 110 years this has proved true for countless patients, yet the paradigm shift to full acceptance in modern health care has yet to occur.

WHAT ABOUT PAYMENT FOR ALTERNATIVE THERAPIES? WHAT'S REASONABLE? WHAT'S FAIR?

Most insurance policies have been written to address treatments provided in the medical model of health care. That is, concerning treatments and therapies designed to suppress symptoms. This may contradict the idea of treating actual causes, or preventing future ill health by proactive means. Is this the most effective way of keeping a population healthy or of decreasing health care costs? If you wait until a minor health issue becomes a major concern the cost to you and your insurance is increased exponentially. Also, to blindly follow the influence of those interested in suppression of symptoms (i.e., through drugs) rather than the elimination or proper management of causes is to allow for gradual health decline, or what appear to be acute episodes of ill health or painful process that actually reflect underlying issues that have been building for long periods.

In the example of chiropractic care, many health insurance policies recognize the value, but place arbitrary allowances based on limited information. As in the case above, it sometimes happens that a patient must choose to pay out of pocket for treatment additional to what's been allowed through insurance. For car crash victims most auto med-pay policies allow for benefits to provide comprehensive treatment. And many people choose to pay cash for chiropractic care because they see it as a quick and reasonable method to relieve pain and maintain health. It doesn't have to be expensive, and it's up to you just how much or how little care you receive at any given time. No one can tell you what to do. You must be a partner with your doctor to assess the options and choose what will serve your best interests now and for the future.

In my experience treating conditions of back and neck pain, headaches, car crash and sports injuries, to name a few, the cost to patients is within a reasonable range. For instance, if a patient shows up soon after (within a day or two) of a new injury or flair-up of old symptoms, they may get well in just one office visit for a cost between $50-$90. If they've waited for many weeks to attend a problem it will take longer and cost more if it becomes difficult to reverse the condition quickly. Certainly the cost is less for conservative care, if that's the right choice, than for testing and treatment in the medical model of health care that may involve multiple tests and doctors to diagnose and treat.

The interest in and application of self care options reflected through Flexible Spending Accounts has allowed for more personal choice in health care, putting some distance between the controlling influence of the insurance contract and that which helps you in any given situation. It's a great boon for you to be able to choose your own doctors and options, especially in the area of complimentary health care that costs less than more common choices. Here's an explanation of these plans: [17]

How Does a Flexible Spending Account Benefit Me?

An FSA saves you money by reducing your income taxes.

The contributions you make to a Flexible Spending Account are deducted from your pay BEFORE your Federal, State, or Social Security Taxes are calculated and are never reported to the IRS. The end result is that you decrease your taxable income and increase your spendable income. You can save hundreds or even thousands of dollars a year.

How Do Flexible Spending Accounts Work?

At the beginning of the plan year (which usually starts January 1st), your employer asks you how much money you want to contribute for the year (there are limits).

You have only one opportunity a year to enroll, unless you have a qualified "family status change," such as marriage, birth, divorce, or loss of a spouse's insurance coverage. The amount you designate for the year is taken out of your paycheck in equal installments each pay period and placed in a special account by your employer.

As you incur medical expenses that are not fully covered by your insurance, you submit a copy of the Explanation of Benefits or the provider's invoice and proof of payment to the plan administrator, who will then issue you a reimbursement check.

What Expenses Are Eligible for Reimbursement?

Any expense that is considered a deductible medical expense by the Internal Revenue Service and is not reimbursed through your insurance can be reimbursed through the Flexible Spending Account. Examples include:

- *Fees paid to doctors, dentists, surgeons, chiropractors, psychiatrists, psychologists, and Christian Science practitioners. Contact lenses and eyeglasses*

- *Fees for hospital services, qualified long-term care services, accident and health, and qualified long-term care insurance premiums, nursing services, laboratory fees, prescription medicines and drugs, and insulin.*

• *Acupuncture treatments*

• *Inpatient treatment at a center for alcohol or drug addiction*

• *Smoking-cessation programs and prescribed drugs to help nicotine withdrawal*

• *False teeth, hearing aids, crutches, wheelchairs, and guide dogs for the blind or deaf*

• *Fees in excess of reasonable and customary amounts allowed by your insurance*

• *Cost of vasectomies, hysterectomies and birth control*

• *Non-elective cosmetic surgery*

• *Co-payments on covered expenses*

• *Deductibles*

• *Braces*

• *Prescription drugs or prescription co-pays*

If you find that you've been unfairly treated by an insurance company or experience denials for services rendered through a valid insurance contract you have the option to contact the Insurance Commissioner in your State (i.e., the Virginia State Corporation Commission Bureau of Insurance) to submit a complaint. They will look into the matter and often influence reversal of unfair decisions made by insurance companies.

HOW YOU CAN KNOW IF THERE'S A PROBLEM BEFORE SYMPTOMS OR PAIN OCCUR

Subtle changes in your body and the way you feel may be early signs of potential trouble. Pain or other symptoms may be the last to appear in certain situations. The use of MRI showed that 66% of people with spinal abnormalities were unaware they had a problem, [18] and in 30% of people who die from a heart attack the first indication that a problem exists is the fatal heart attack itself. If you pay close attention and make appropriate changes in your lifestyle, or seek out preventive care that addresses specific issues, your need for medical intervention will be minimal. Consequently cost reflects that foresight. The focus on appropriate lifestyle changes as we age, and the pursuit of proven methods to effectively reverse the effects of early physical problems contributes to quality of life and longevity.

Most people don't realize where most of the energy from the brain is dedicated to maintain life. Brain research demonstrates that it requires only 10% of the brain's energy to run all the systems and functions of the body (circulatory, muscular, nervous system, etc.) The other 90% of the brain's energy is absorbed in the millions of constant calculations necessary to balance and control where we are in time and space. [19] This makes sense if you think about it for a moment: One of the most important survival functions is the flight response, the ability to run away from predators (in the primitive sense). Therefore, we must be able to instantly orient in time and space to make the judgments that allow survival. The input for this ability is through the joints and nerves to the spine and brain (as sensory *input* to establish 'orientation' or 'position') then out again from brain to nerves to joints to maintain or change orientation, the motor *output* that provides for movement. This is technically called "proprioception," a function of your nervous system. As an example, consider what happens if you're standing. Your brain is receiving information that the knees are locked, responding with appropriate impulses to the muscles (motor '*output*') to maintain posture. If someone comes from behind and unlocks your knee the input and output instantly change. You feel as if you'd fall until you lock the knee again. This is one explanation of the way we work in chiropractic: By changing the input through the small joints along the spine the brain responds by relaxing muscle spasms in the neck or back that contribute to pain, radiation of pain or numbness. That's why relief is often instantaneous when the right procedure is applied.

According to Dr. Roger Sperry, Nobel Prize recipient for brain research, 90% of the stimulation and nutrition to the brain is generated by movement of the spine. This is analogous to a windmill generating electricity. The cerebrospinal fluid that nourishes the brain and spinal cord is contained within the cranium and the spinal canal. It requires movement to force that fluid through the channels and maximize the way those sensitive structures are maintained in good health. Obviously, any obstruction along the spine or compromise to spinal movement is an obstruction to nourishing the brain and nervous system. This is why a health maintenance approach to prevent health problems is so often recommended by holistic doctors, chiropractors, osteopaths, nutritionists and others.

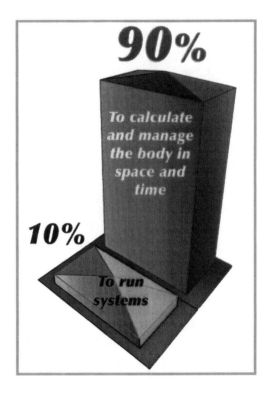

A simple way to detect a problem:

The brain gets 85% of the information to monitor your position in space and time from the eyes. The other 15% comes from joint position, especially the intricate system of moveable segments in your spine. If your spine is healthy (no misalignment, arthritis, scoliosis, pathlogy or subluxation present) and the information flowing to and from the brain is not impeded, you should be able to stand on one foot with your eyes closed for about 22 seconds without losing your balance. [20]

CASE HISTORY #5:
SKEPTICISM TURNS TO JOY WHEN PAIN IS GONE IN ONE TREATMENT

George H., at a young 26 years, suffered from back pain localized to the lower back, with numbness in his left leg that came and went unpredictably. When he showed up in my office one of his main concerns was staying active, especially with his favorite pastime, kayaking. He had just four weeks before he was off to travel around the country for the summer, kayak strapped to the top of his car, before beginning business school in the fall. He said "I didn't believe in chiropractors, but a friend got well and I wanted to go to the person she trusts."

We took two x-rays of George's lower back and found a very slight pinching of the last disc in his spine. It was clear on the x-ray that the nerve there would be vulnerable to painful pressure, and I explained to George that we could reverse that trend now while in the early stages and at his young age, keeping him active, if he would agree to a few treatments over three or four weeks. He was happy to do so, and we began on the first day by giv-

*ing George therapy to relax muscles, and the chiropractic
adjustment to relieve pressure on the nerve directly.*

*Two days later George arrived for his second appoint-
ment with a report that he was 100% better. He couldn't
believe it, and insisted on showing me how he could lean
backward without pain after just one treatment. George
was no longer a skeptic, and I explained to him that although there's been a lot of negative propaganda against
my profession and other competitive complimentary approaches in health care, it's not a matter of "belief." There
are scientific explanations for the effects of certain procedures and modalities. In his case the gentle adjustment of
just one segment of his spine relieved pressure and changed
the input/output around the muscles of his lower back. It
takes a little mind bending sometimes to get away from
the deeply entrenched conditioning of our modern era. An
open mind goes a long way in learning about and access-
ing what are effective alternatives to drugs and surgery.*

IS THERE ANY DANGER TO "ALTERNATIVE" APPROACHES IN HEALTH CARE? WHAT YOU SHOULD KNOW

Very often we hear about pharmaceutical drugs
causing harm. Surgery can cause damage that's irre-
versible. And sometimes patients become infected

while in the hosptial. Consider that an estimated 2 billion prescriptions are written in the U.S. every year earning $49 billion for the pharmaceutical industry. A 13 year study by the U.S. Office of Public Health found that two thirds of all over-the-counter drugs do not do what the manufacturers report. [21] Over 190,000 deaths per year were the result of drug toxicity and 300,000 deaths (the fourth leading cause of death in the U.S.) was from hospital acquired (iatrogenic) infections. [22] There are 8.8 million prescription related hospitilizations costing $47 billion annually; 28% of hospital admissions are due to prescription side effects. [23] It's common knowledge, too, that the overuse of prescription drugs leads to viral and bacterial mutations with drug resistance and increased dangers associated with infections.

Surgery can be a life saver. Over 50 million surgeries are performed in the United States each year. But it was reported on ABC's Nightline that 30% (15 million) of all surgeries are unnecessary and that 60,000 people die each year from unnecessary surgery.

A specific reflection of these statistics is in the malpractice premuims paid by various doctors and health care providers. Higher premiums reflect higher risk. USA Today reported that malpractice insurance premuims for obstetrics and gynecology jumped to $80,000 a year, [24] and premiums for a typical internal medical doctor will run between $10,000 and $20,000 or more, depending on specialty and history of incidents. [25]

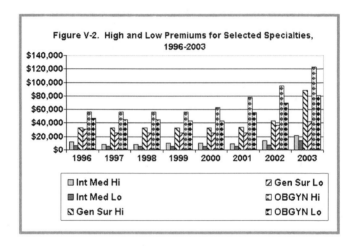

Figure V-2. High and Low Premiums for Selected Specialties, 1996-2003

Compare that with what chiropractors pay in malpractice.

"Most consumers don't realize that common over-the-counter drugs for neck pain and headaches–the conditions often treated by chiropractic cervical manipulation–are hundreds of times more likely to cause serious reactions, such as gastrointestinal bleeding, liver damage, or even

death, than the drug-free chiropractic approach to these conditions...

The low risks of chiropractic treatment are reflected in the extremely low malpractice rates for the nation's doctors of chiropractic. Malpractice insurance rates for health care professionals across the country are directly proportional to the number of claims made against those particular groups by patients. According to NCMIC, one of the nation's largest chiropractic malpractice insurance companies, the insurance rate for doctors of chiropractic across the country is $1,500. For general physicians, rates range from $10,000 to $20,000–depending on the area of the country." [26]

Competition being what it is, some groups exaggerate or misrepresent ideas about various products or services to hold an edge in the market. It's unfortunate, but true. Every so often we see a story about the dangers of a particular treatment or vitamin supplement, for instance. But where do these stories come from and are they statistically valid? You should be allowed to choose for

yourself and determine just what will serve
you best without propaganda influencing
your decisions. And it is you who must be
responsible and feel good about your choice
to enjoy the highest benefit. Self serving motives often influence the way a story is told.

Important questions to ask a doctor or surgeon:

1. Is this drug/surgery/treatment really necessary? Is it going to help? If so, how?
2. Are there any complications or side effects to consider?
3. How often have you treated this condition? What's your success rate?
4. Will you perform the treatments/ surgery yourself or an associate?
5. How long should I expect to recover, and how long until I'm back to my normal routine?
6. What can I do to help myself?
7. What would happen if I choose not to have this treatment/ surgery/drug?

SELF CARE MADE SIMPLE: KEEP MOVING

A revolution's occurred in the U.S. over the past few decades. You could label it a "raging phenomenon." It's called "exercise." It's become fashionable to jog, bike, skate, swim, golf, dance, strengthen and kickbox our way to better health. Baby boomers account for the majority of this trend: At 76 million strong, baby boomers are very resistant to the lifestyles of their aging parents. [27] With good reason too: The negative effects of a sedentary lifestyle, antequated eating habits, dependence on medication and a medical model of health care have taken a toll. Despite the advertisements to the contrary, we know intuitively that using drugs that have a long list of potential side effects is not nature's way of handling health issues. The pain in your stomach, for instance, does not reflect a lack of "purple pill" in your blood stream. What do you think happens, by the way, if you take a powerful antacid, counteracting the natural mechanism of digestion? Is it possible the food doesn't break down, making it's way to the intestines undigested to putrify in your gut causing other trouble (i.e., diverticulisits and a need for other drugs or even surgery)?

This is one example of the model of treating symptoms only and what can happen as a result.

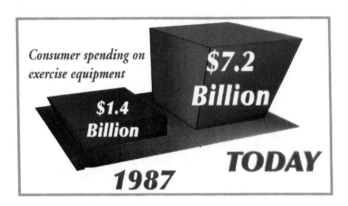

Exercise has been proven to:

1. Reduce cancer
2. Reduce heart disease
3. Reduce diabetes
4. Improve circulation
5. Lower blood pressure
6. Increase energy
7. Improve brain function
8. Improve mood
9. Help manage weight
10. Promote better sleep

It's been shown that regular exercise has a positive effect on brain chemistry which can positively effect mood and happiness. Regular exercise programs in companies reduce the cost of health care, insurance and can improve productivity. If we consider all the benefits of regular exercise it's hard to ignore that a little goes a long way to support health and reduce costs within the health care system. Using the example of cancer, we can see just how exercise benefits.[28]

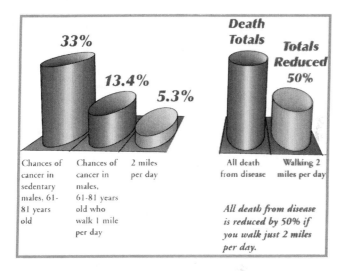

33%	13.4%	5.3%	Death Totals	Totals Reduced 50%
Chances of cancer in sedentary males, 61-81 years old	Chances of cancer in males, 61-81 years old who walk 1 mile per day	2 miles per day	All death from disease	Walking 2 miles per day

All death from disease is reduced by 50% if you walk just 2 miles per day.

Longer life expectancy is the result of hundreds of different factors and subtle improvements in our circumstances. Garbage collection alone has probably saved millions of lives over time. Knowledge of medicines, nutrition, exercise and preventive measures will likely increse life span even further. But we're challenged by processed and fatty foods, stress, pollution, depletion of minerals in our soil and other modern day problems. This may explain why certain diseases have increased (i.e., heart disease and cancer) that were anomalies at the beginning of the twentieth century. It's estimated that 68% of cancers are caused by lifestyle choices (tobacco, foods, sedentary lifestyles, etc.). You can do something about it by making choices, even small ones, along the lines that are discussed here, and self educating for lasting good health.

DOES THE COST OF STAYING HEALTHY HAVE TO BE HIGH?

As I write this book we know a woman who's turning 98. She's doing well, active on a daily basis and mentally alert. If you saw her you'd think she might be 70 at most. She's an inspiration for those who aspire to a long and happy life. I'm looking forward to her 100th birthday party.

With life expectancy increasing dramatically, it's likely that you and I might also reach the ripe age of 90 or more. Millions of baby boomers are looking to retirement with hopeful enjoyment of many decades of quality living. Have we, though, planned for the future reasonably and with enough foresight that we'll be able to stay healthy without exorbitant cost? Many prospective retirees are shocked by how much they may have to spend on health care even if they qualify for Medicare. It's estimated that with premiums for supplemental health insurance and unexpected needs costs can rise to hundreds or thousands of dollars a month during retirement years. "People are beginning to realize that funding retirement means budgeting additional amounts to pay rising medical costs." [29] The landscape of health care for the future is changing rapidly, rising costs reflecting, in my view, a misunderstanding of approaches that truly prevent and support health before crises arise.

Medicare falls short when it comes to providing benefits for the elderly. With myriad sectors of the health care marketplace vying for Medicare dollars, the entitlements that many retired persons looked forward to are potentially unavailable. Providers, too, feel the limits of Medicare as congress looks for ways to cut costs, decrease reimbursements, and impose contraints on the ways in which doctors can receive fair compensation for services rendered. As with most insurance, the model on which Medicare is based, and has been lobbied to develop policy, is the medical model of treating symptoms. Hidden causes, or subtle symptoms that presage more serious health concerns, are ignored.

Therefore, payments are made only for those conditions that demonstrate the required seriousness to "justify" cost. This does not reflect research into various ways in which health can be promoted and maintained over time, those that cost much less than the usual approaches. For example, if certain physical structures are out of alignment the whole body breaks down. The disease process called osteoarthritis is a reflection of such breaking down as parts of the skeletal system wear out from abnormal mechanical pressure. Therefore people who pursue preventive care to maintain good body alignment have fewer of those problems and live longer healthier lives in general.[30] It's valuable for everyone who considers and pursues options other than the constant taking of pills to cover up symptoms (that might be trying to tell you something important).

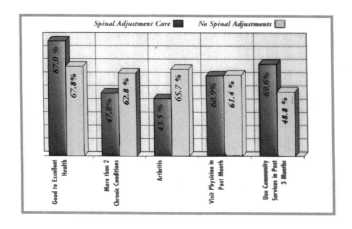

CASE HISTORY #6:
53 YEAR OLD RUNS A MARATHON WITH HELP FROM CHIROPRACTIC CARE

While training for a marathon, a hobby of his, Charlie S. began feeling severe back pain that made it impossible to run. He was distraught when he arrived in my office, with only two weeks until the big day. X-rays of Charlie's lower back showed several degenerated discs, probably caused by the pounding of running over many years combined with some misaligned bones in his spine. Charlie didn't want to stop running, though, and I promised to do everything I could to get him out of pain and keep him active for a long time to come. But he had to agree to several things first.

Degenerative disc disease is common as we age, the spinal discs become dehydrated (technically termed "dessication"), and vulnerable to physical stress. I advised Charlie to dramatically increase his intake of water while we began treating his back pain aggressively, seeing Charlie every day for the two weeks before the marathon. For Charlie we introduced gentle traction along with the chiropractic spinal adjustment for best results. He was to perform specific stretching exercises in between treatments too.

After a few days Charlie was able to try a short run, which went well. Each day he increased the distance until the day of the marathon, which he successfully ran without pain. He was most grateful for our help that his goal could be met. Because he wants so much to stay active Charlie comes in every two months for a "tune up" with an adjustment to relieve any pressure that may have built up in the lower back as he runs. This allows him to pursue his hobby without restriction, the idea being to prevent further decay of discs or osteoathritic change as well as we're able. Charlie is, so far, very happy with the result.

Solutions To A Health Care Crisis: The "United States Health Corp" And The "Naturopath General" (Or "What I'd Do If I Were President")

Conflicting interests and misinformation drive any circumstance to confusion. Solutions are then difficult to come by. So it is in our healthcare system now. Politicians are trying to figure out how to solve what may be an unsolvable problem. Or is it?

We certainly don't solve any problem by imposing what's not worked before. Sometimes we have to come up with completely new models for the future. As I said earlier, it seems contradictory to allow insurance companies to contract with everyone, pretending that this gives "universal" coverage. It only gives the insurance companies a pile more money and the possibility to control what people are allowed. That's not universal.

What I propose is that we initiate a United States Health Corp, somewhat modeled after the Peace Corp. In my imagining, people who want to become health care providers are sought out and screened for a compassionate nature and appopriate mental and emotional qualities. These men and women, most likely young, would be provided tuition for necessary education to achieve their goal, then be required to serve in areas of the U.S. that need health care for a defined period of time (say, four to six years). The available fields would include internal medicine, surgery, nursing, chiropractic, osteopathy, mental health, podiatry, geriatric and other specialites and subspecialties. After their service they would be invited into the private health care system and given preference for jobs in hospitals and established practices, or for loans to begin private practice. This model would provide the care needed to the underserved and uninsured while giving back life enhancing lessons to those who participate.

Regarding another issue, the head of the United States Public Health Service is called the Surgeon

General. A surgeon is defined as "a physician qualified to treat those diseases that are amenable to or require surgery." The paradigm of health care, model of disease, and influences that a surgeon is receptive to are very different than those that would influence many other health care providers and differing paradigms. As mentioned above, chiropractic and medicine have a long history of disagreements. In the U.S. we have a perceptual divide in health care that imposes a model on all rather than evaluating specific and individual need. I see this as analogous to what would happen if we had just one political party: There would be no debate and no opportunity to shift with the times and move ahead with some sense of enlightenment (at least that's the theory).

Naturopathy is defined as "a system or method of treating disease that employs no surgery or synthetic drugs but uses special diets, herbs, vitamins, massage, etc. to assist the natural healing process." With an idea to balance the debate and provide a public health forum for information and education, I propose also that we estalish the **Naturopath General** along side the Surgeon General. Both offices would provide a public health service, integrating the best approaches from each without narrow identification to an antequated scientific model. We can no longer simply suppress symptoms or cut out disease, we must see it as part of the whole person and treat accordingly. I wonder, though, how open the medical associations and pharmacuetical companies would be to this idea. What do you think?

Conclusion

We all want quality of life as long as we live. As life expectancy increases it becomes imperative that we take responsibility to learn and apply that which has the most potential for our families and ourselves. No one else will do it for us, and when considering options we must beware of conflicts of interest that mislead. If we know that a particular lifestyle change or treatment has the potential to provide more quality of life in specific ways and without side effects then, individually and collectively, we must demand that it remain available to us. By doing so and allowing for the flow of information in an integrated way, you can assess what's best for any circumstance. The function of your doctors, like me, is to support your decisions and provide quality care that prevents future problems and gives you the best chance to stay alive and well. My advice: Be a Self-Directed Patient now.

"One generation's miracle may be another's scientific fact. Do not close your eyes to acts or events that are not always measureable. They happen by means of inner energy available to all of us.
—Bernie Siegel, M.D.

Footnotes:

[1] *The Rainmaker* by John Grisham (novel) and the movie directed by Francis Ford Coppola

Appealing and Preventing Denied Claims by Simon Rosenstein

[2] http://www.ohioinsurance.gov

[3] resource4thepeople.com

[4] Dr. Robert P. Lynch, Portland, Maine (as reported in an ACA news release, April 12, 1996)

[5] * U.S. Dept. of Commerce, ** Market Enterprises Inc., Tampa FL, 1996 & U.S. Statistical Bulletin April – June 1995 (refers to "Non-surgical treatment for back pain").

[6] www.beloit.edu/~nutritio/doctors.htm

[7] drtomt.blogspot.com/2007/09/chiropractors-solution-to-health-care.html

[8] Senate Document Number 264: U.S. Department of Agriculture

[9] *Inventing Disease and Pushing Pills: Pharmaceutical Companies and the Medicalisation of Normal Life*, by J. Blech.

[10] U.S. Department of Commerce

[11] Fred Fiske Commentary, National Public Radio, March 13, 2008

[12] *Desktop Guide to Complimentary and Alternative Medicine*, by Edzard Ernst

[13] http://www.rxlist.com/cgi/generic/prampex_ad.htm

[14] Waler Last, http://users.mrbean.net.au/~wlast/meridians.html

[15] http://en.wikipedia.org/wiki/Wilk_v._American_Medical_Association

[16] James Swanton, Albert Einstein College of Medicine, New York

[17] http://financialplan.about.com/cs/insuranc1/a/Flex SpendPlan.htm

[18] San Francisco Chronicle, July 14, 1994

[19] Dr. Roger Sperry, Nobel Prize recipient for brain research.

[20] UCLA study on the eyes and brain

[21] Good Housekeeping, April 1996

[22] National Center for Health Statistics, Vital Statistics Report

[23] USA Today, April 1, 1997

[24] USA Today, January 18, 2004

[25] George Coppolo, Chief Attorney, OLR Research Report: 2003-R-0662

[26] Dr. Donald J. Krippendorf, letter to WCVB-TV, 12/1/2003

[27] American Sports Data, Inc.

[28] New England Journal of Medicine, #338 p. 94-95

[29] Bob Ericson, Uncommon Wisdom (Wachovia Securities), Issue no. 5

[30] Top Clinic Chiro 1996: 3(2): 46-55

APPENDIX ONE
Curriculum Vitae

Patrick John McNally

Doctor of Chiropractic
435-A Carlisle Drive
Herndon, Virginia 20170
703 481-1616
drmcnally@myvitalcare.com

An experienced Chiropractic Physician
specializing in non-surgical relief of musculoskeletal
pain syndromes. Extensive knowledge related to back
and neck pain, headaches, sciatica, radiculopathies
(pinched nerves), numbness and tingling, disc herni-
ation, degenerative spinal conditions, sports and car
crash injuries. Wellness care and counseling also offered. A published author with good communication
skills. His policy: No patient turned away without all
questions answered.

Comprehensive Education and Fully Qualified

Bachelor of Science, Psychology: 1981   James Madison University
                                          Harrisonburg, Virginia

Bachelor of Science, Biology: 1983   National College of Chiropractic
                                          Lombard, Illinois

Chiropractic Internship: 1984-85   NCC Patient & Research Ctr.
                                          Lombard, Illinois

Doctor of Chiropractic Degree: 1985   National College of Chiropractic
                                          Lombard, Illinois

Certified by the
National Board of Chiropractic Examiners: 1985
Licensed by the
Virginia Board of Medicine: 1985
Licensed by the
Maryland State Board of Chiropractic Examiners: 1985
Certified in
Physical Therapy, MD State Board: 1985

Professional Experience

Chiropractic Physician: As owner and director of The Elden Street Back and Neck Pain Center from 1986 to 2003, thousands of patients have been accepted and treated for myriad conditions within the scope of practice defined by the Virginia Board of Medicine. In 2003, the practice was renamed Vital-Care™ with a direction to engage more closely patients and their needs, and diversification of services available. This effort continues to evolve in today's challenging healthcare marketplace. The theme of all service to patients is to invite full participation and informed choice when pursuing options in support of health, active living and longevity. The bias is to non-surgical and holistic approaches in the support of life.

Professional consultant: During years 2006 and 2007 Dr. McNally began New World View Coaching, engaging doctors from around the United States in a discussion of changes in health care and how to support ethical, transformative means of growing and succeeding individually and collectively. This effort brought many insights into the difficulties experienced by providers challenged within the restriction imposed by insurance contracts, Medicare and limited options in health care today. Pursuing deeper understanding, Dr. McNally replaced that concept with

New Life View, a service provided in workshop environments to people interested in understanding how collective experience and the connections between people influence health, happiness and success. New Life View is a generic service not restricted to a singular profession or community. All are invited to experience through these workshops the insights that may be available.

Memberships and Associations

American Alternative Medical Association
American Chiropractic Association
Association for Integrative Health Care Practitioners
American Holistic Medical Association
Association for Comprehensive Energy Psychology

Published Books and Articles

How to Stay Alive and Well Despite Your Doctor, Your Insurance Company and Your Government, 2008, Word Association Publishers.

Is Bert Hellinger's "Constellation Approach" Energy Psychology?: A Perspective on Morphic Resonance, 2007, Association for Energy Psychology Newsletter

Systemic Energetics: Finding an Effective Therapeutic Position, 2008, Association for Energy Psychology Newsletter

APPENDIX TWO

Insurance Companies That Currently
Provide Policies Including Chiropractic
Care And Possible Allowance For
Additional Complimentary Medicine

Accordia National
Aetna PPO
Aetna HMO
Anthem BCBS
BCBS Federal
Carefirst BCBS
CIGNA
COURESOURCE
Gallagher Benefit
Great West
GUARDIAN
Humana-Choice
Mailhandlers
Medicare
Mutual of Omaha
NCAS
NCPPO
Principal Life
Unicare
United HealthCare

* If your insurance is not on the list, out of network benefits
  may apply.

**Attention Personal Injury (car crash) victims: You may be el-
igible to assign benefits to receive care with no out of pocket
cost to you.

APPENDIX THREE

SAMPLE FOOD LIST FOR IMPROVED HEALTH AND WEIGHT MANAGEMENT

(for reference: not intended to replace the advice
of your medical doctor, nutritionist or other
professional health care provider)

Every year I try to read one or two books on foods and their qualities. The first realization from this effort is that there's a lot of opinion, often contradictory information, too much generic application, and a great deal of potential confusion about various foods and their properties.

That being said, there is value to understanding principles regarding the foods we eat and how to combine them. What I've done here is cross reference four sources: 1. The Yeast Syndrome by Trowbridge; 2. Lists of alkaline or acidic foods; 3. The glycemic index and glycemic load tables; and 4. Lists of foods that are acid binding, tending to decreased mucous production. These lists are imperfect and limited, but we can extrapolate information from them. This is developed from the list of foods that bias toward vegetarian (including dairy products) and pescetarian (including fish). You may choose other foods to add or delete from this list, and can reference the sources for more information to suit your specific needs.

Here's what you need to know:

1. The **Phases (I-IV)** indicate, from least to most, those foods that contribute to yeast and bacteria overgrowth in the body. Staying in the first phase for a few weeks, then moving to second, third and fourth as health issues improve is the idea. You might choose from the first and second phases for a time to improve health, that way allowing for more choices than being too strict. If you really want to improve health and lose weight stay in **Phase I**, but know too that this list is not customized

for you and your needs. There are more foods (i.e., of the carnivorous variety) on the lists in the references that might be appropriate for you.

2. Alkaline foods are in **bold**, acidic in ***bold italics***. Those that I could not identify are in plain text. It's best to stay on the alkaline side of foods, that being more health giving than becoming too acidic. Many health issues are attributed the acidic nature of the American diet. It's not possible or necessary to completely avoid acidic foods, but to choose more often the alkaline. To have fish or meat in a meal (acidic) with an abundance of broccoli (alkaline) is more balanced than to have meat and acorn squash (both acidic), for example.

3. GI/GL index is indicated next to the foods like this: 46/9. Glycemic index is the immediate effect on blood sugar levels of a particular food. A glycemic index of less than 55 is desirable. But keep in mind that my list does not indicate serving size. A whole bag of potato chips is obviously worse than a handful. Glycemic load is the relative tendency of a food to keep the blood sugar level high. The higher the numbers in this regard the worse for health. It's possible to have a high GI but reasonably low GL. Not all foods have been studied in this regard, and the lists are limited. But again, we can extrapolate a bit. GL of 10 or less is low (best), 11-19 intermediate, 20 or more is high. Keeping to the lower GI/GL index demonstrates weight loss and lower blood sugar levels.

4. The idea of acid binding foods that decrease the tendency to mucous in the body may be new to you, and the lists are not extensive, but I've indicated here those foods with an asterisk (*). The idea is that there's a range in which foods fall that either do or do not promote mucous production. The less the better and healthier, in this regard.

So, to stay with foods that don't promote yeast or mucous, have a low GI/GL and are alkaline is the best thing to do. If you try, you'll eat like a bird and have painful cravings. But if you use this list to your advantage and education you can likely prevent or reverse some health conditions (i.e., overweight, cholesterol, blood sugar and other issues).

Phase I – IV: lesser to higher for yeast promoting foods

Alkaline +/-
Acidic +/-

GI of 55 is low; GL of 10 is low (i.e. 46/13)

* = Acid binding or tending to less mucous

PHASE I

VEGETABLES:

Alfalfa sprouts
Artichoke, Chi.*
Asparagus*
Bamboo sprouts
Banana pepper
Endive
Bean sprouts
Bell pepper, green
Cabbages:*
Bok Choy*
Broccoli* 0/0
Cauliflower* 0/0
Collard greens 0/0
Head, green, red
Kale 0/0
Savoy 0/0
Carrot 47/3
Celery* 0/0
Carrot juice 43/10
Celeriac
Cucumber* 0/0
Curly cress
Dandelion* 0/0
Dulse
Eggplant
Fennel
Garden cress 0/0
Garlic
Jalepeno pepper
Jicama
Kelp
Leek
Lettuces:* 0/0
Butterhead* 0/0
Celtuce* 0/0
Iceberg* 0/0
Loose-leaf* 0/0
Arugula* 0/0
Romaine* 0/0
Roguette* 0/0
Mung bean sprout
Onion*
Okra
Parnsip
Pumpkin*
Rape
Radish*
Sweet red pepper
Sea Kale
Shallot

Spinach* 0/0
Squahes: 0/0
Acom
Banana
Cheese
Pumpkin*
Spaghetti
Etc, all...
String bean
Swiss chard
Tomatillo
Tomato*
Turnip greens
Water celery
Watercress*
Belgian endive
Yucca

HERBS:

Allspice
Anise
Apple mint
Basil
Bergomot
Boneset tea*
Borage
Burdock root tea*
Caraway
Cardamom
Celery seed
Chamomile (tea)
Chive
Clove
Coriander
Cumin
Dill*
Fenugreek
Ginger
Ginseng (tea)
Hibiscus (tea)
Horeradish
Lavender
Lemon balm
Licorice
Marjoram
Menthol
Mint
Nutmeg
Oregano
Paprika
Parsley
Peppercorn

Peppermint
Pimento
Rosemary
Saffron
Sage
Savory
Sorrel
Spearmint
Tarragon
Thyme
Tumeric
Vanilla
Misc.:
Aloe vera
Green tea*
Ground cherry
Guava
Herbal teas*
Ruhbarb*
Safflower oil
Salt
Sunflower oil
Sunflower seed
Tamarind

ANIMAL PRODUCTS:

Eggs 0/0
Milk
Butter
Yogurt 33/11
Goat cheese/milk*
Crab 0/0
Lobster 0/0
Shrimp 0/0
Clam 0/0
Squid 0/0
Albacore tuna 0/0
Anchovy 0/0
Cod 0/0
Eel 0/0
Flounder 0/0
Halibut 0/0
Mahi-mahi 0/0
Monkfish 0/0
Sea bass 0/0
Sea trout 0/0
Swordfish 0/0
Tuna 0/0
Salmon* 0/0
Trout 0/0

PHASE II

VEGETABLES:	
Artichoke, globe*	
Artichoke, jer. 0/0	
Avocado 0/0	
Brussel sprouts*	
Water chestnuts	
Mustard greens	
Green pea 50/3	
Black-eyed p 46/13	
Garb., dried 28/8	
Garb., can 42/9	
Split pea 32/6	
Peas/green* 48/3	
Potatoes*	
Baked 90/26	
Mashed 77/15	
French fr. 75/22	
Soy products*	
Tofu	
Soy bean* 20/1	
Soy milk 44/8	
Green tea*	
Ground cherry	
Guava	
Herbal teas*	
Ruhbarb*	
Safflower oil	
Salt	
Sunflower oil	
Sunflower seed	
Tamarind	

FRUITS:

Melons (most)
Watermelon * 80/4

GRAINS:

Corn oil
Cornmeal 68/9
Corn starch
Popped corn 72/8

Wheat germ
Wild rice

MISC.:

Bay leaf
Capers
Cayenne pepper
Cinnamon
Mustard seed
Olives*
Red pepper
Sassafras
Sesame oil/seed
Tabasco
Tahini

ANIMAL PRODUCTS:

Cheeses: 0/0
Cream cheese 0/0
Colby 0/0
Edam 0/0
Gouda 0/0
Monterey jack 0/0
Whey cheese
Honey

PHASE III

VEGETABLES:	
Beans, dried	Pine nuts

FRUITS:

VEGETABLES:	FRUITS:
Adzuki	Apples 40/6
Black 30/7	Blackberry
Fava	*Blueberry*
Great northern	Boysenberry
Green	Cherry 22/3
Kidney 23/6	Crabapple
Lima 32/10	*Cranberry 52/16*
Mung 31/5	Kumquat
Navy 44/12	Lemon
Pinto 39/10	Lime
Carob	Longberry
Hearts of palm	Papaya 60/17
Lentils 29/5	Peach 50/5
Beets/greens*	Pinapple 66/6
Beets can* 64/5	Pomegranate
Sweet corn 60/20	Rosehips
Grains (most)	Strawberry 40/1
Barley	Tangelo
Buckwheat	Wineberry
Grits	Youngberry

	MISC.:
Millet	
Oats	Apple pectin
Rye	Arrowroot
Wheat	Coffee*
Bran	Wintergreen
Bulgur	
Flour	**ANIMAL PRODUCTS:**

NUTS:

NUTS:	ANIMAL PRODUCTS:
	Cottage cheese
	Other cheeses:
Almond 0/0	*Cheddar 0/0*
Beechnut	*Parmesan 0/0*
Chesnut	*Romano 0/0*
Filbert	*Reggiana 0/0*
Hazelnut	*Mozzarella 0/0*
Peanut	*Provolone 0/0*
Peanut oil	*String 0/0*
Pine nut	
Pinyon	

PHASE IV

FRUITS:

Apricot 33/10
Banana 56/12
Cantaloupe 65/4
Cherry 22/3
Coconut
Date 103/42
Fig 65/16
Grape 48/8
Grapefruit 25/3
Mango 55/9
Nectarine
Orange 42/5
Pear 38/4
Persimmon
Plum 42/5
Prune 32/10
Raisin 70/28
Rasberry

VEGETABLES:

Agave
Mushroom
Tapioca
Taro root
Yam* 40/13
Yuca

SUGARS:

Beet
Cane
Corn (syrup)
Honey 57/10
Maple syrup
Molasses

NUTS:

Brazil 0/0
Cashews 22/3
Hickory
Litchi
Macadamia 0/0
Pecan 0/0
Pistachio
Walnut

MISC.:

Apple cider

Yeast
Black tea
Brewer's yeast
Chocolate
Cocoa
Cocoa butter
Hops
Pickles
Vinegar

CHEESE:

Asiago 0/0
Bleu 0/0
Brick 0/0
Brie 0/0
Camembert 0/0
Gorgonzola 0/0
Gruyere 0/0
Muenster 0/0
Roquefort 0/0
Stilton 0/0
Swiss 0/0

MISC. FOODS:

Popcorn 72/8
Pot. Chips 55/11
Lentil soup 44/9
Minestrone 40/7
Tomato soup 40/6
Black bean 64/17
Green pea 66/27
Split pea 60/16
Choc. Bar 49/?
Sauerkraut
Wakame
Spirulina
Tamari
Tempeh
Whey protein
Scallops
Peanuts 14/1
Peanut butter
Almond milk
Olive oil
Canola oil
Flax oil
Corn oil
Avacado oil

Butter
Choc. Milk 39/9
Rye, pump.* 41/5
Baked potato* 76/23
Spaghetti 40/16
Pancake 67/39
White rice 64/23
Brown rice 55/18
Lentils 29/5
Choc. cake 40/20
Croissant 67/17
Scones 105/8
Cranberry ju. 55/16
Grapefruit ju. 48/11
Orange ju. 52/13
Tomato ju. 40/4
Bagel 72/25
Oat bran bread 50/9
Whole wh. br. 73/10
Pita bread 57/10
Sourdough rye 48/6
All bran 38/9
Basmati rice 62/22
Rice hi. amyl. 40/15
Rye crisp. 64/11
Wheat thins 67/12
Ice cream 60/8
Yoghurt 40/9
Canned peach 65/11
Pineapple juice 46/15
Pizza thin 58/12
Fettucine (egg) 36/15
Corn chips 72/18
Life savers 73/21
Fish sticks 38/7
Hamburger bun 61/13
Salmon sushi 48/17
Minerals
Pita bread 57/10
Wheat tortilla 30/8
Pomegranate ju. 67/23
Blueberry ju. 58/14
Grape ju.* 58/24
Porter*
Ale*
Some white wines*

APPENDIX FOUR
Bibliography

Suggested Reading To Inform And Support Free Choice In Health Care

*Critical Condition: How Health Care in America Be
came Big Business—and Bad Medicine,* by
Donald L. Barlett and James B. Steele_

*You Have An Ugly Baby: The unpleasant truth about
your company's health care cost and how you
CAN change your destiny,* by Daniel Rickard

*The Serpent on the Staff: The Unhealthy Politics of the
American Medical Association,* by Howard
Wolinsky and Tom Brune

Appealing And Preventing Denied Claims, by Simon
Rosenstein

*Inventing Disease and Pushing Pills: Pharmaceutical
companies and the medicalisation of normal life,*
by J. Blech

*Selling Sickness: How the World's Biggest Pharmaceuti
cal Companies Are Turning Us All Into Patients,* by Ray Moynihan and Alan Cassels

*Our Daily Meds: How the Pharmaceutical Companies
Transformed Themselves into Slick Marketing
Machines and Hooked the Nation on Prescrip-
tion Drugs,* by Melody Petersen

The Food Revolution: How Your Diet Can Help Save Your Life and Our World, by John Robbins

The China Study: The Most Comprehensive Study of Nutrition Ever Conducted and the Startling Implications for Diet, Weight Loss and Long-term Health, by T. Colin Campbell and Thomas M. Campbell II

McDougall's Medicine: A Challenging Second Opinion, by John A. McDougall

The Spectrum: A Scientifically Proven Program to Feel Better, Live Longer, Lose Weight, and Gain Health, by Dean Ornish

Arthritis Relief: Breakthroughs in Natural Healing, by Deborah L. Wilcox

Love, Medicine and Miracles : Lessons Learned about Self-Healing from a Surgeon's Experience with Exceptional Patients, by Bernie S. Siegel, M.D.

Spark: The Revolutionary New Science of Exercise and the Brain, by John J. Ratey

Fresh Start: The Stanford Medical School Health and Fitness Program, Stanford Center for Research in Disease Prevention

The Schwarzbein Principle: The Truth About Losing Weight, Being Healthy, and Feeling Younger, by Diana Schwarzbein, M.D.

Syndrome X: The Complete Nutritional Program to Prevent and Reverse Insulin Resistance, by Jack Challem, Melissa Diane Smith, and Burton Berkson M.D.

The New Glucose Revolution Shopper's Guide to GI Values 2008: The Authoritative Source of Glycemic Index Values for More Than 1,000 Foods, by Jennie Brand-Miller, Kaye Foster-Powell, and Fiona Atkinson

APPENDIX FIVE

Internet Resources for Informed Options in Health Care Today

(INFORMATION PROVIDED TO SUPPORT SELF CARE OPTIONS AND CHOICE IN HEALTH CARE; OPINIONS MAY NOT REFLECT THOSE OF THE AUTHOR DIRECTLY)

WEBSITE ADDRESS	THEME OR IDEA PROMOTED
http://myvitalcare.com	Website for Vital Care and Dr. McNally's practice
http://www.advocatelawgroup.com	Advocates for people victimized by Insurance Bad Faith
http://www.scc.virginia.gov	Virginia State Corporation Commission links to Virginia Bureau of Insurance
http://www.burtongoldberg.com	"The Voice of Alternative Medicine"
http://www.drnorthrup.com	"Mother Nature vs. Father Pharmaceutical"
http://www.naturalsolutionsmag.com	"Dedicated to Natural Remedies and Healthy Solutions"
http://www.resource4thepeople.com	With links to issues of Insurance Bad Faith
http://nccam.nih.gov	National Center for Complimentary and Alternative Medicine
http://www.altmedicine.com	Alternative Health News Online
http://www.amerchiro.org	The American Chiropractic Association
http://www.joinaama.com	American Alternative Medical Association
http://www.holisticmedicine.org	American Holistic Medical Association
http://www.acupuncture.com	"Gateway to Chinese medicine"
http://www.acupuncture.com	The Ingham Method of Reflexology
http://abchomeopathy.com	Homeopathic information and products
http://www.amtamassage.org	American Massage Therapy Association
http://www.acefitness.org	American Council on Exercise